Brighty
Fox

This book belongs to :

_____

First Edition: October 2024

Dépôt légal, Bibliothèque et Archives nationales du Québec, 2024

https://brightyfox.com/contact-me

Contact me at

Welcome, Future Giggle Masters!

Hey there, future laugh legend!

Welcome to the silliest, most laugh-out-loud book you'll ever read!

Get ready for endless giggles with everything you need to become a joke-telling superstar:

Jokes Galore: This book is packed with hilarious jokes, ready for you to share the laughs with family and friends.

Lunchbox Joke Cards & Wacky Constraints:

- Lunchbox Joke Cards: Scan the QR code to download these joke cards as a PDF, or feel free to photocopy and share for daily laughs in every lunchbox!

- Wacky Constraints: Use these cards to add funny twists to jokes—whether from random jokes on the page, the book, or lunchbox cards. For extra fun, spin the Giggle Wheel online!!

Reaction Tracker: Pick a random joke from the page, add the constraint, and rate it with a smiley face at the end!

Are you ready to become the king or queen of giggles?

Turn the page, and let the fun begin!

Jokes Galore !

Welcome to the ultimate joke collection!

Get ready to discover tons of funny, wacky,
and totally giggle-worthy jokes.

Flip through, find your favorites, and get ready
to laugh out loud!

These jokes are perfect for sharing with friends,
family, or anyone who needs a good laugh.

Why was the math book sad?

Because it had too many problems.

What do you call a sleeping dinosaur?

A dino-snore!

Knock knock.
Who's there?
Lettuce. Lettuce
who? Lettuce in,
it's cold outside!

What do you call an alligator in a vest?

An investigator!

What's red and bad for your teeth?

A brick!

Why did the peanut go into space?

HA HA HA HA

He wanted to be an astro-nut!

8

WHY DID THE TOMATO TURN RED?

Because it saw the salad dressing!

WHY DID THE COFFEE FILE A POLICE REPORT

It got mugged!

Why do bananas wear sunscreen?

So they don't peel!

9

It goes chew chew!

How does a train eat?

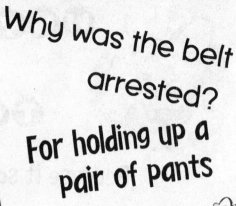

Why was the belt arrested?

For holding up a pair of pants

Knock knock,
Who's there?
Boo.
Boo who?
Don't cry, it's just a joke!

Why do fish live in saltwater?

Because pepper makes them sneeze!

What do you call cheese that isn't yours?

Nacho cheese!

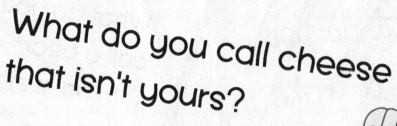

What did the baby corn say to the mama corn?

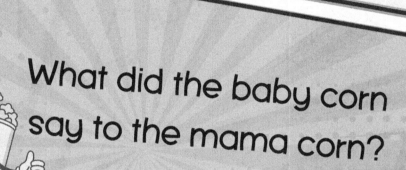

Where's popcorn?

Knock knock. Who's there? The interrupting cow. The interrupting... MOOOOOOO!

11

What do you call a fake noodle?

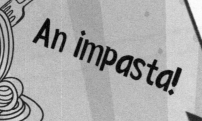

An impasta!

What do you call a bear with no teeth?

A gummy bear!

Knock, knock! Who's there? Lettuce. Lettuce who? Lettuce in, it's cold outside.

What do you call birds falling in love

Tweet hearts

What do you write in a rabbit's birthday card ?

Hoppy birthday!

Knock, knock!
Who's there?
Eyesore.
Eyesore who?
Eyesore do love you.

13

What are ten things you can always count on?

Your fingers

How do you get a squirrel's attention?

Act like a nut

Knock, knock!
Who's there?
Figs. Figs who?
Figs the doorbell

What kind of shoes do ninjas wear?

SNEAKERS!

What did the left eye say to the right eye?

Between us, something smells!

Why don't cats like online shopping?

They prefer a cat-alogue.

Knock, knock!
Who's there?
Deja vu.
Deja vu who?
Knock knock!

15

What do you call a cold dog ?

A chili dog

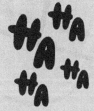

What do you call a lazy baby kangaroo?

A pouch potato

Why is it so hard for a leopard to hide ?

HA HA HA HA HA

Because it's always spotted

16

What did one toilet say to the other?

You look flushed.

HA HA HA!

LOL

Why was the equal sign so humble?

Because it wasn't greater than or less than anyone else.

Knock, knock! Who's there?
Tank.
Tank who? You're welcome.

17

Why did the strawberry cry?

Because its parents were in a jam

Why did the cell phone get glasses?

It lost all its contacts

Knock, knock!
Who's there?
Says.
Says who?
Saysme!

What kind of tree fits in your hand?

A palm tree

Do you know what's odd?

Every other number

Why did the golfer bring extra pants?

In case he got a hole in one!

Knock, knock!
Who's there?
Woo.
Woo who?
Glad you're excited, too.

Why did the skeleton go to the party alone?

HA HA HA

Because he had no body to go with!

How do bees get to school?

A school buzz.

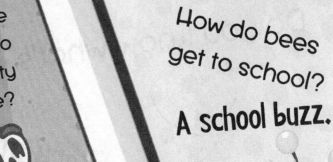

Why don't crabs donate to charity?

Ha Ha Ha Ha Ha Ha

Because they are shellfish

Which knight created the round table?

Sir Cumference

What do you call an anxious mosquito?

A jitterbug

Knock, knock!
Who's there?
Orange.
Orange who?
Orange you going to let me in?

21

What did the volcano say to the other?

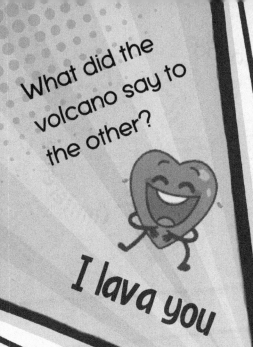

I lava you

How many blueberries can you grow on a bush?

All of them

Knock, knock.
Who's there?
Needle.
Needle who?
Needle little help right now!

What does a clam do on his birthday?

He shellabrate

How do you make seven an even number?

Remove the S

What do you cakes and baseball have in common?

They both need a batter

Knock knock.
Who's there?
Cargo.
Cargo who?
Car go beep beep!

23

What tool is most helpful in a math classroom?

Multi-pliers

What do clouds wear under their clothes?

Thunder-wear

What has a head and tail but no body?

A coin

24

What did the mom ower say to the little ower?

Hi, bud!

What kind of award did the dentist receive?

A little plaque

Knock knock.
Who's there? Spell.
Spell who?
W-h-o

25

What tables don't require any math? .

HAHAHA

Dinner tables

Why did the chicken get a job?

Because she was tired of being cooped up!

Knock knock.
Who's there?
Pecan.
Pecan who?
Pecan somebody your own size!

What's a vampire's favorite fruit?

A blood orange!

Where will you find Friday before Thursday?

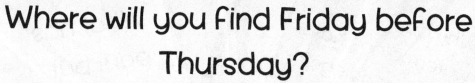

A dictionary

What do elves learn in school?

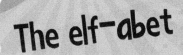

The elf-abet

Knock knock.
Who's there?
Yoda lady.
Yoda lady who?
I didn't know you could yodel!

Why do watermelons have fancy weddings?

Because they cantaloupe

What has ears but cannot hear?

A corn eld

How did the cabbage win the race?

HA HA HA

It was a-head

28

What did the triangle say to the circle?

You're pointless

What did the horse say after it tripped?

Help! I've fallen and I can't giddyup!

Knock, knock.
Who's there?
Water.
Water who?
Water you doing today?

29

Why can't you hear a pterodactyl going to the bathroom?

Because the "P" is silent

What do you call a well-balanced horse?

Stable

LOL!

Knock, knock.
Who's there?
Ice cream.
Ice cream who?
ICE CREAM SO YOU CAN HEAR ME!

What do you call an angry carrot?

A steamed veggie

30

How do you make an egg-roll?

You push it!

What do you call a pile of cats?

A meow-ntain

Knock, knock.
Who's there?
Weirdo.
Weirdo who?
Weirdo you think you're going?

What would bears be without bees?

Ears

Time flies like an arrow.

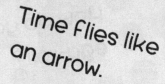

Fruit flies like a banana

I ordered a chicken and an egg online.

HAHA HA

I'll let you know what comes first

A soccer match

What lights up a soccer stadium?

What do lawyers wear to court?

Lawsuits

Knock, knock.
Who's there?
Avenue.
Avenue who?
Avenue knocked on this door before?

33

What do sprinters eat before they race?

Nothing. They fast

What has more lives than a cat?

LoL

A frog, because it croaks every day

Knock, knock.
Who's there?
Howard.
Howard who?
Howard you like to sit outside in the cold while someone keeps asking, "Who's there?"

What do you call a pig that practices karate?

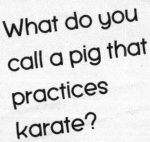

A pork chop

34

What has four wheels and flies?

A garbage truck!

Why can't you trust the king of the jungle?

LOL

Because he's always lion

Knock knock.
Who's there?
Adorable.
Adorable who?
A-door-a-bell don't work,
that's why I knocked!

35

What do you call a sad strawberry?

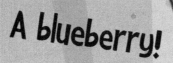

A blueberry!

How do you organize a space party?

You planet

What do cows read the most?

HA HA HA HA HA HA

Cattle-logs

36

I lost an electron.

You really have to keep an ion them!

LOL

What did O say to 8?

"Nice belt"

Knock, knock.
Who's there?
Venice.
Venice who?
Venice your dad coming home?

What did the drummer name her twin daughters?

Anna 1, Anna 2

What's small and red and has a rough voice?

HAHA!

A hoarse raddish!

Knock, knock.
Who's there?
You.
You who?
Yoo-hoo!
Anybody home?

Why shouldn't you tell secrets in a cornfield?

Too many ears

What does a spy do when he is cold?

He goes undercover

How does the moon cut his hair?

HA HA

Eclipse it

Knock, knock.
Who's there?
Watson.
Watson who?
Watson on TV in there?

39

When do computers overheat?

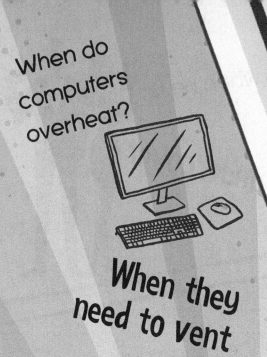

When they need to vent

What do you call a sad cup of coffee?

Depresso

What did the cucumber say to the pickle?

HA HA HA HA

You mean a great dill to me

40

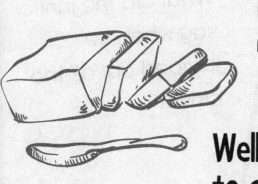

Did you hear the rumor about butter?

Well, I'm not going to go spreading it!

What goes up and down but doesn't move?

Stairs

Knock, knock.
Who's there?
Lena.
Lena who?
Lena little closer
and I'll tell you!

41

What do you call a magician that looses his magic?

Ian

What did the janitor say when he jumped out of the closet?

Supplies!

Knock, knock.
Who's there?
Ben.
Ben who?
Ben knocking for 10 minutes!

Hat did the yoga instructor say when her landlord tried to evict her?

Namaste

42

Why did the kid stock up on yeast?

He wanted to make some dough

What did the football coach say to the broken vending machine?

Give me my quarterback

Knock, knock.
Who's there?
Izma
Izma who?
Izma lunch ready yet?

43

Why is Peter Pan always flying?

Because he Neverlands

Why did an old man fall in a well?

Because he couldn't see that well!

Knock, knock.
Who's there?
Theodore.
Theodore who?
Theodore wasn't opened, so I knocked

How do you tell the difference between a bull and a cow?

It is either one or the udder!

Why are peppers the best at archery?

Because they habanero!

HAHA

Knock, knock.
Who's there?
Yvette.
Yvette who?
Yvette is a doctor for animals.

What do you call a chicken that is staring at a lettuce?

Chicken sees a salad

Which bear is the most condescending?

A pan-duh!

What do you call a blind dinosaur?

A do-you-think-he-saw-us

LOL!

Knock, knock.
Who's there?
Nana.
Nana who?
Nana your business!

47

Why aren't koalas actual bears?

They don't meet koalafications

LoL

Why can't you play hockey with pigs?

They always hog the puck

Knock, knock.
Who's there?
Pudding.
Pudding who?
Pudding your shoes on is important if you want to come outside!

What kind of dog tells time?

A watch dog

How do you identify a bald eagle?

All his feathers are combed over to one side

Knock, knock.
Who's there?
Butter.
Butter who?
Butter let me in or I'll freeze!

Why does a tiger have stripes?

So he will not be spotted

What starts with gas and has three letters?

A car

What do you call a funny mountain?

HAHA!

Hill-arious

Knock, knock.
Who's there?
Stew.
Stew who?
Stew cold out here, let me in!

How does a cow do math?

HAHA!

With a cow-culator!

Where do polar bears keep their money?

A snow bank

Knock, knock.
Who's there?
Curry.
Curry who?
Curry me home will you!

What room can no one enter?

A mushroom

What did one colored egg say to the other?

Heard any good yolks lately?

Haha, that's egg-cellent!

Knock, knock.
Who's there?
Olive.
Olive who?
Olive you sooooo much!

What kind of key can never unlock a door?

LOL

A monkey

54

Why did Santa go to music school?

So he could improve his wrapping skills

What do you call an old snowman?

HA HA HA HA

Water

Knock, knock.
Who's there?
Soup.
Soup who?
Superman!

What are the strongest days of the week?

Why did they bury the battery?

Saturday and Sunday. Every other day is a weekday

Because it was dead

Why did Mozart sell his chickens?

They kept saying, "Bach, Bach, Bach"

What word starts with E and has only one letter in it?

LOL!

Envelope.

How many tickles does it take to make an octopus laugh?

HA HA HA

Ten tickles

Knock, knock.
Who's there?
Onion.
Onion who?
Onion mark, get set, go!

What's another name for a clever duck?

Wise quacker!

What nails do carpenters hate hammering?

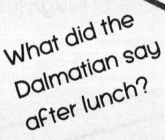

Fingernails

Knock, knock.
Who's there?
Alpaca.
Alpaca who?
Alpaca the trunk, you pack the suitcase.

What did the Dalmatian say after lunch?

That hit the spot!

59

What does garlic do when it gets hot?

It takes its cloves off!

What kind of dog does a magician have?

A Labracadabrador!

What do frogs order at fast-food restaurants?

HA HA HA

French flies!

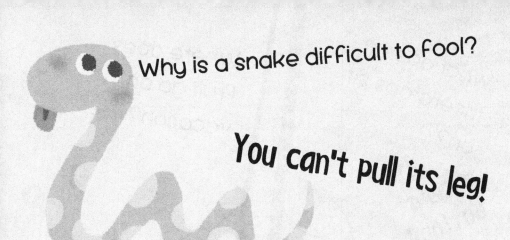

Why is a snake difficult to fool?

You can't pull its leg!

What did the dog say when it sat on sandpaper?

"Ruff!"

Knock, knock.
Who's there?
Geese.
Geese who?
Geese what I got in the mail today?

61

What does a triceratops sit on?

Its tricera-bottom!

Where does fruit go on vacation?

Pear-is!

Knock, knock.
Who's there?
Toucan.
Toucan who?
Toucan play at this game!

Why can't you trust tacos?

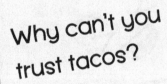

Because they always spill the beans!

Why couldn't the angle get a loan?

Because his parents wouldn't cosine!

What kind of keys do kids prefer?

Cookies!

Knock, knock.
Who's there?
Rhino.
Rhino who?
Rhino every knock knock joke
there is, so there's no use in
telling any more.

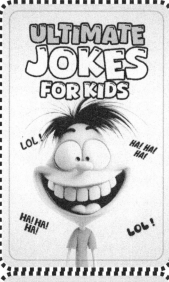

1

Why can't your nose
be 12 inches long?

(Because then it would
be a foot !)

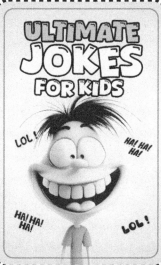

2

What do you call a
sleeping bull?

(A bulldozer !)

3

Why did the cookie go
to the doctor ?

(Because it felt
crummy !)

4

Why do cows have hooves instead of feet ?

(Because they lactose !)

5

Why did the student eat his homework?

(Because the teacher said it was a piece of cake !)

6

What did one plate say to the other plate ?

(Lunch is on me !)

7

What do you get when you cross a vampire and a snowman ?

(Frostbite !)

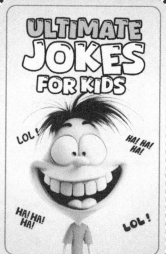

8

Why was the computer cold ?

(Because it left its Windows open !)

9

Why did the chicken cross the playground ?

(To get to the other slide !)

10

What do you get when you throw a lot of books into the ocean ?

(A title wave .)

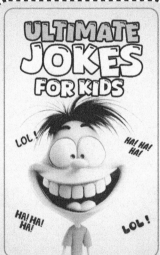

11

What do you get if you cross a fish with an elephant ?

(Swimming trunks !)

12

Why did the music teacher leave her keys in the piano ?

(Because that's where they belong !)

13

Why don't skeletons go trick or treating ?

(Because they have no body to go with !)

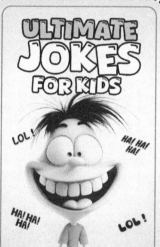

14

What's a skeleton's least favorite room ?

(The living room !)

15

Why did the cow go to outer space ?

(To see the moooon !)

16

Why couldn't the bicycle stand up ?

(Because it was two tired.)

17

What has two legs but can't walk ?

(A pair of pants.)

18

Why was six afraid of seven ?

(Because seven eight nine.)

19

Why are fish so smart ?

(Because they live in schools !)

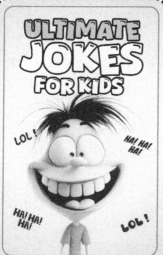

20

What did one hat say to the other ?

(Stay here, I'm going on ahead.)

21

How do you make a lemon drop ?

(Just let go of it !)

22

Why do birds fly
south in the winter ?

(It's faster than
walking !)

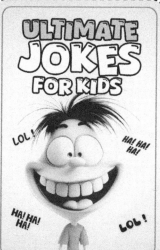

23

Why did the chicken go
to the playground ?

(To get to the other
slide !)

24

What is a snake's
favorite subject in
school ?

(Hissstory.)

25

Why did the picture go to jail !

(It was framed !)

26

Why do seagulls fly over the sea?

(Because if they flew over the bay, they'd be bagels.)

27

Why are ghosts such bad liars ?

(Because they are too transparent.)

28

What kind of room
has no doors or
windows ?

(A mushroom.)

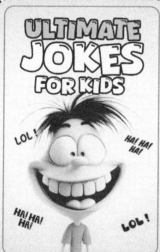

29

Why don't skeletons
fight each other ?

(They don't have the
guts.)

30

Why did the banana go
to the doctor?

(It wasn't peeling
well).

31
How does the ocean say hi ?

(It waves !)

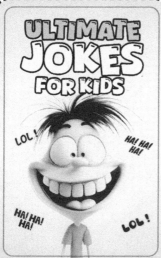

32
Why was the broom late ?

(It swept in !)

33
How do you fix a broken pumpkin ?

(With a pumpkin patch.)

What is brown and
sticky ?

(A stick !)

Why can't you give Elsa
a balloon ?

(Because she will let it
go !)

What did one wall say
to the other ?

(I'll meet you at the
corner !)

37

Why did the
computer get sick ?

(It had a virus.)

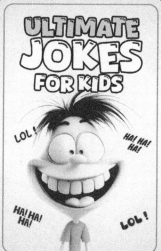

38

What do rabbits eat
for breakfast?

(IHOP)

39

How does a scientist
freshen her breath ?

(With experi-mints !)

40

Why did the man run around his bed ?

(Because he was trying to catch up on his sleep !)

41

What time is it when an elephant sits on your fence ?

(Time to get a new fence !)

42

What's the king of the classroom ?

(The ruler !)

43

Why did the chicken
join a band ?

(Because it had the
drumsticks !)

44

What kind of haircuts
do bees get ?

(Buzzzz cuts !)

45

Why did the cow jump
over the moon ?

(To get to the Milky
Way !)

46

Why don't oysters share their pearls ?

(Because they are shellfish !)

47

Why did the spider surf the web ?

(To catch some bugs.)

48

Why don't eggs tell jokes ?

(Because they might crack up !)

49

What do you call a
pig that does
karate ?

(A pork chop !)

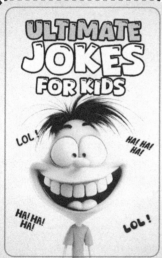

50

What is a bat's
favorite sport ?

(Baseball)

51

Why did the bikes get
detention at school?

(They spoke too much)

52

Where do pencils come from ?

(Pennsylvania)

53

What does the Invisible Man drink at snack time ?

(Evaporated milk)

54

What does a pickle say when he wants to play cards ?

("Dill me in!")

Challenge the Comedian!

Think you're good at telling jokes?

Let's see how funny you can be with a twist!

Use the Constraint Cards to add a silly challenge to each joke—whether it's from the book or the Lunchbox Joke Cards.

Scan the QR code p.65 to download a printable PDF or feel free to photocopy the cards. Then, draw a card to find out if you need to tell the joke like a robot, a chicken, or in slow motion.

For a super surprise, spin the Giggle Wheel online to keep the laughs coming!

CONSTRAINTS

1

Tell the joke... like you just ate a lemon!

CONSTRAINTS

2

Tell the joke... while pretending you're on a rollercoaster!

CONSTRAINTS

3

Tell the joke... as if you're talking to an alien!

4

Tell the joke... while balancing something on your head!

5

Tell the joke... as if you have a balloon voice!

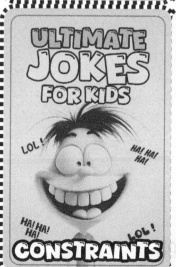

6

Tell the joke... while pretending you have no teeth!

CONSTRAINTS

7

Tell the joke... as if you're trapped in a bubble!

CONSTRAINTS

8

Tell the joke... while acting like a chicken!

CONSTRAINTS

9

Tell the joke... as if your feet are stuck in glue!

10

Tell the joke... while pretending your pants are on fire!

11

Tell the joke... while pretending you're a monkey!

12

Tell the joke... as if you're running in slow motion!

Get Ready to Giggle!

To add some extra fun to your jokes, explore the page where random jokes and the Giggle Wheel await! Each click reveals a new joke, and you can spin the wheel for funny constraints to make your joke-telling even more exciting. Just scan the QR code or enter the link below to access both features.

Happy joking!

https://brightyfox.com/giggle-wheel

Rate the Reaction!

Ready for a challenge?

Choose a joke from the page indicated, then tell it with the funny constraint provided!

After delivering the joke, mark your audience's reaction by checking one of the five faces.

Let's see which jokes get the best laughs!

Challenge	Chose a joke from page	constraints Tell the joke...	Reaction				
#1 ☐	10	like you just ate a lemon!	☐	☐	☐	☐	☐
#2 ☐	15	as if you're talking to an alien!	☐	☐	☐	☐	☐
#3 ☐	12	while pretending you're on a rollercoaster!	☐	☐	☐	☐	☐
#4 ☐	7	while balancing something on your head!	☐	☐	☐	☐	☐
#5 ☐	17	as if you have a balloon voice!	☐	☐	☐	☐	☐
#6 ☐	20	as if you're trapped in a bubble!	☐	☐	☐	☐	☐
#7 ☐	11	while pretending you have no teeth!	☐	☐	☐	☐	☐
#8 ☐	27	while pretending your pants are on fire!	☐	☐	☐	☐	☐
#9 ☐	49	while acting like a chicken!	☐	☐	☐	☐	☐
#10 ☐	18	as if you're running in slow motion!	☐	☐	☐	☐	☐
#11 ☐	28	while pretending you're a monkey!	☐	☐	☐	☐	☐
#12 ☐	15	as if your feet are stuck in glue!	☐	☐	☐	☐	☐
#13 ☐	56	with you eyes closed	☐	☐	☐	☐	☐
#14 ☐	34	in a whisper	☐	☐	☐	☐	☐
#15 ☐	21	like a robot	☐	☐	☐	☐	☐
#16 ☐	46	while hopping on one foot	☐	☐	☐	☐	☐
#17 ☐	52	using a spooky voice	☐	☐	☐	☐	☐
#18 ☐	14	as if you're singing an opera	☐	☐	☐	☐	☐
#19 ☐	33	with your mouth full of water (pretend only!)	☐	☐	☐	☐	☐
#20 ☐	8	in slow motion	☐	☐	☐	☐	☐
#21 ☐	37	while pretending to juggle	☐	☐	☐	☐	☐
#22 ☐	23	in a deep monster voice	☐	☐	☐	☐	☐
#23 ☐	16	as if you're a pirate	☐	☐	☐	☐	☐
#24 ☐	19	while dancing	☐	☐	☐	☐	☐
#25 ☐	9	like you're underwater	☐	☐	☐	☐	☐

Challenge	Chose a joke from page	constraints Tell the joke...	Reaction				
			😭	😣	🤓	😎	🤪
# 26 ☐	24	as fast as you can	☐	☐	☐	☐	☐
# 27 ☐	50	like you're a magician	☐	☐	☐	☐	☐
# 28 ☐	47	backwards (start with the punchline)	☐	☐	☐	☐	☐
# 29 ☐	30	in a silly accent (e.g., French, British, or cowboy)	☐	☐	☐	☐	☐
# 30 ☐	35	while acting like you're scared	☐	☐	☐	☐	☐
# 31 ☐	20	while pretending to cry	☐	☐	☐	☐	☐
# 32 ☐	25	like a superhero	☐	☐	☐	☐	☐
# 33 ☐	29	in slow motion and then super fast	☐	☐	☐	☐	☐
# 34 ☐	41	with a big smile on your face	☐	☐	☐	☐	☐
# 35 ☐	26	while pretending you're on a tightrope	☐	☐	☐	☐	☐
# 36 ☐	53	while clapping your hands after every word	☐	☐	☐	☐	☐
# 37 ☐	38	as if you're a news reporter	☐	☐	☐	☐	☐
# 38 ☐	42	while hiding behind a chair or table	☐	☐	☐	☐	☐
# 39 ☐	55	in a super squeaky voice	☐	☐	☐	☐	☐
# 40 ☐	45	while pretending to be an alien	☐	☐	☐	☐	☐
# 41 ☐	36	like you're reading a bedtime story	☐	☐	☐	☐	☐
# 42 ☐	39	while standing on your tiptoes	☐	☐	☐	☐	☐
# 43 ☐	48	like you're a rock star	☐	☐	☐	☐	☐
# 44 ☐	54	while pretending to be a cat	☐	☐	☐	☐	☐
# 45 ☐	32	as if you're very sleepy	☐	☐	☐	☐	☐
# 46 ☐	30	in a royal king or queen's voice	☐	☐	☐	☐	☐
# 47 ☐	43	while pretending to conduct an orchestra	☐	☐	☐	☐	☐
# 48 ☐	51	while doing a robot dance	☐	☐	☐	☐	☐
# 49 ☐	31	in a high-pitched chipmunk voice	☐	☐	☐	☐	☐
# 50 ☐	44	while pretending to be a sneaky ninja	☐	☐	☐	☐	☐

Table Of Contents

119

Wait, There's More!

Want an Extra Jokes Bonus ?

You can get extra bonus jokes as a thank-you gift!
Just ask a grown-up to help you leave a review for
this book.

Once they help you write the review, scan the QR code
below and share the proof. I'll send your bonus fun
straight to your email!

Keep exploring and having fun!

Contact me at
https://brightyfox.com/contact-me

Brighty
Fox

https://brightyfox.com/unlock-bonus

SCAN ME

121

Explore Another Fun Adventure
with
Brighty Fox!

Brighty Fox

Made in the USA
Las Vegas, NV
09 December 2024

13603259R00069